COMMUNAL SOCIETIES IN AMERICA
AN AMS REPRINT SERIES

HISTORY AND CONSTITUTION OF THE I
COMMUNITY

AMS PRESS
NEW YORK

THE IOWA JOURNAL OF HISTORY AND POLITICS

HISTORY AND CONSTITUTION OF THE ICARIAN COMMUNITY

BY

ETIENNE CABET

TRANSLATED

BY

THOMAS TEAKLE

THE STATE HISTORICAL SOCIETY OF IOWA
IOWA CITY IOWA
1917

Library of Congress Cataloging in Publication Data

Cabet, Étienne, 1788-1856.
History and constitution of the Icarian Community.

(Communal societies of America)
Reprint of an article originally published in the Iowa, journal of history and politics, v .15, 1917.
1. Icarian Community. I. Title.
HX653.C23 1975 335'.9'77343 72-2962
ISBN 0-404-10726-5

Original pagination has been maintained

Reprinted from the edition of 1917, Iowa City
First AMS edition published in 1975
Manufactured in the United States of America

AMS PRESS INC.
NEW YORK, N.Y. 10003

HISTORY AND CONSTITUTION OF THE ICARIAN COMMUNITY

HISTORY AND CONSTITUTION OF THE ICARIAN COMMUNITY

[An interesting chapter in the history of Iowa is the story of the Icarian colony in Adams County. The following pages contain a translation of a small book of ninety-six pages, entitled *The History of the Colony or Republic of Icaria in the United States of America,* written by Etienne Cabet, the founder of the Community. The copy which was used was of the second edition published in Paris in 1855. The book was found in the library of the Historical Department of Iowa at Des Moines. While only incidentally touching upon the existence of the colony in Iowa, the material in the following pages furnishes the necessary background for the history of the colony in this State.— THOMAS TEAKLE]

A GENERAL IDEA OF THE ICARIAN COLONY.

The Icarian Colony in America was founded for the purpose of clearing, cultivating and subduing the wilderness, while establishing there all useful industries for the production and manufacture of all that is needed for a people; of creating a State; of creating first one Commune, then others successively; of procuring the well-being of all while working; of offering an asylum for the proscribed Republicans who may adopt its principles while combining the necessary qualities and conditions for membership; of making an experiment, in the interest of Humanity, to determine the best system of political and social organization which will be the most favorable to progress and the most capable of securing the happiness of the Human Race.

To accomplish these ends, *the system of the Icarian Colony* (applied to a country called *Icaria* in the work published under the title of a *Journey in Icaria*) appears to be the best. It is the system that will be tried at first.

This colony does not resemble any other since it has for

its purpose not alone the interest and happiness of its members but also that of humanity as a whole.

It is planned that it shall be neither exclusively French nor German, American nor English. It is *Universal,* in the sense that it admits emigrants from all countries, provided they adopt its principles, its system, its social contract or constitution and laws, and agree to the conditions of admission explained hereafter.

In discussing the Colony, there will first be related a few facts concerning the history of the Community and the preparative station at Nauvoo up to the present time. Next will be given a general idea of the Icarian system as it seems to be adapted either to a State or a Commune. Then the Icarian Constitution will be discussed as well as the law respecting the General Assembly, together with the conditions, form and effect of admission. Finally, in a separate prospectus, will be indicated the precautions to take either in preparing for the journey or for the *trip* from Europe to America.

CHAPTER I.

SOME FACTS CONCERNING THE HISTORY OF ICARIA.

CONVERSION TO COMMUNISM.

During an exile of five years, from 1834 to 1839 (for having said that the system of Louis Philippe would inevitably lead to bloodshed and ruin), Cabet gave all his time, while in London, to the writing of works which he believed were the most useful to the People. During this time he wrote three short, popular histories — a *Universal History,* a *History of England,* and a *History of the French Revolution.*

History exhibits on every page only disorders and calamities. Cabet sought for the cause and the remedy as well. He saw the *cause* in a *bad social organization,* and the *remedy* in a *better one.*

Seeing everywhere and always the war between *Aristoc-*

racy and *Democracy,* he decided that, in order to establish peace, it would be necessary to abolish one of the two belligerents, giving the preference to *Democracy.* And as he saw nowhere a great organized *Democracy,* he sought for a means of organizing a nation in the form of a Democracy.

He soon found it to be impossible to organize a Democracy with *opulence* and *poverty,* with rich and poor and with inequality of fortune. Thus he became convinced that it was impossible to establish equality of fortune, plenty and happiness without *Community of Property.*

He then tried to organize, on paper, a great Community (a Commune, a State). He was soon convinced that Communism would completely solve all social questions; that it was realizable, possible and even easy if one willed it; that it would realize immense *savings* and greatly increase *production;* while it would assure plenty, well-being and happiness for all citizens and all men.

He consulted all ancient and modern philosophies and went through all the great philosophic works in the great Library of London. He discovered with as much joy as surprise that all, with Christ at the head, admitted that *Communism* was the best social system. He then wrote his *Journey in Icaria.*

JOURNEY IN ICARIA.

This is a relation of an imaginary journey, much like Plato's *Republic,* John's *Apocalypse,* Augustine's *City of God,* Thomas More's *Utopia,* or Campanella's *City of the Sun.*

Though in the form of a *Journey* or of a *romance,* it is in reality a description of the political and social organization of the Community. It is further a *scientific and philosophical treatise* couched in the most obvious, intelligent and popular form.

The work is divided into three parts.

Part I.— The first 6 chapters contain the actual dangers and pleasures of the Journey in Icaria; a glance at the towns, the roads, the inns, the country, the political and social organization, and a description of Icaria, the capital.

Chapters 7 to 16 treat of the food, dress, homes, and Education; of the Organization of labor and industry; of health, doctors and hospitals; of writers and men of learning, judges, lawyers, etc.; and of women's workshops and the romans[?].

Chapters 17 to 19 concern Agriculture and Commerce.

Chapters 20 and 37 deal with Religion.

Chapters 21 to 26 treat of the political Organization and newspapers.

Chapters 15 and 27 are concerned with marriage.

Chapters 28 to 35 relate to recreations, theatres, holidays and games.

Chapter 40 concerns women in general.

Chapters 36 to 42 concern the relations of the colonists and foreigners.

Part II.— The first 3 chapters discuss the faults of the old political and social Organizations.

Chapters 4 to 6 treat of the establishment of the Community within an old society and of the transitory régime.

Chapters 7 and 8 contain a statement of objections that have been made to the Icarian plan, together with their refutation.

Chapters 9 and 10 contain a historical description of the progress of Democracy and Equality.

Chapter 11 contains a view of the development of industry.

Chapters 12 and 13 contain the opinions of Philosophers concerning the Community.

Chapter 14 contains a discussion of the future welfare of Humanity.

Part III.— The Doctrines and Principles of the Community.

In order to prove that Icarian Communism is the same thing as Christianity, Cabet wrote the *True Christianity.*

TRUE CHRISTIANITY.

This work is divided into 2 parts.

The *1st part* or *introduction* explains the religious ideas held by the first *Peoples,* the Egyptians, the Hebrews and Moses with something of the history of the Jews and of John the Baptist.

The *2nd part* contains:— A glance at the history of Jesus Christ from His birth to His preaching; His *teaching* concerning God, the reign of God, Brotherhood, Equality, Liberty, Democracy, Unity, Association, wealth and poverty, work and wages, community of goods.

It also contains the *Ethics* of Christ — His ideas upon the future life, His *Religion* and His *Creed.*

It has also a relation of His preaching, triumph, anguish, and resurrection; the story of the Apostles, their Communism, their writings — Gospels and Epistles; some comments upon the Church Fathers; and finally an identification of Communism with Christianity.

OTHER WORKS OF CABET.

Upon returning from exile, Cabet published his popular History of the French Revolution (in 4 volumes), 6 political pamphlets dealing with the crisis of 1840, together with five pamphlets against prisons and the bombardment of Barcelona.

Later, he published from 30 to 40 pamphlets to explain further his Icarian Communism. Among these were: Why I am a Communist; My Communistic Creed; 12 Letters of a Communist to a Reformer concerning the Community; My Proper Path; The Citizen's Guide; The Communistic

Propaganda; Woman; The Laborer; Status of the Social Question; Short Popular Discussions; The Icarian Almanac, since 1843; the newspaper, the Populaire, since 1841.

For the purpose of refuting all objections, criticisms, and attacks, he published the Refutation of the Friend of Mankind; The Refutation of the Workshop; Refutation of the Abbe Constant; Democracy becomes Communism in Spite of Itself; The Challenge to Communism; Safety or Ruin; The Social Cataclysm; The Whole Truth for the People; The Veil Lifted; The Mask Torn Away; Down with the Communists; The Inconsistencies of Lamennais; Water upon Fire, a Reply to Carmenin; Biography of Citizen Cabet.

Since 1848, he has published Good and Evil, Danger and Safety; Eleven Talks on fraternal Society; The Insurrection of June; The Realization of the Community; A Letter to the Archbishop of Paris; Two Letters to Louis Napoleon; My Trial and My Acquittal.

PROPAGANDA.

Convinced that such a Communistic system based on Brotherhood could not be set up through violence and compulsion, Cabet adopted, after the example of Christ, a lawful and pacific propaganda. He wished the Community to be established through persuasion, conviction and the free consent of the individual. He addressed himself only to public opinion. He exhorted the people to renounce secret societies, plots, mutiny and insurrection, clinging only to self-improvement and moral reflection, for the purpose of preparing themselves for the life of the Community.

This doctrine of the Icarian Community and of Brotherhood, this lawful and peaceful propaganda, was completely successful as was attested by its having more conversions than any other teaching of the day.

After only six years of propagandist writing, the mass of

the working classes, especially in the large cities, and the best of the workers in each industry, became Icarians.

And if the Government had permitted Cabet to give talks or oral and public explanations in the popular assemblies, either in Paris or in the departments as was granted the Fourierists, there is scarcely any doubt that the population today would be generally converted to Icarian Communism.

And even if he had been granted the permission to try the Community in France, he certainly would have found all the Icarians and money necessary to found one or many Icarian Communities in France, and the problem of the suppression of misery, pauperism and the proletariat would have been solved.

PERSECUTION.

But the Government, the Aristocracy, the privileged classes, the guardians of the old abuses, and the higher clergy, aligned themselves for the purpose of slandering and persecuting the Icarians, as formerly the Pharisees and Pagans had slandered and persecuted the Christians.

The revolutionary party itself, especially the *National* party and the one of *Reform,* united with the enemies of the Icarians to slander and persecute them on account of their *lawful and peaceful* propaganda.

While the first proscribed the Icarians as revolutionists, the second proscribed them as anti-revolutionists.

EMIGRATION TO AMERICA.

Then, to avoid this general persecution, Cabet invoked, in May, 1847, these words of Jesus Christ to his disciples: "If they persecute you in one city, go you into another."

And he proposed emigration for the courageous purpose of founding Icaria in an American wilderness.

The founding of Icaria in America, on the other side of the seas, two or three thousand leagues away, in a new climate, in a waste region where all would need to be created, side by side with men of an alien tongue, would be a more costly and difficult enterprise than it would have been in France.

The proposition also raised many objections and much opposition. But Cabet replied to all: "Nothing can frighten or dissuade the Icarians, who will heed only their *devotion* to Humanity." Upon February 3, 1848, there left for Texas (where more than a thousand acres of ground had been granted to the north-west along the Red River) the first Advance Guard, comprising seventy men, whom Cabet greeted with the title *Soldiers of Humanity,* entrusted with exploration, selection and preparation.

Other similar Advance Guards were to follow the first at fortnightly intervals. The families of the members of the Advance Guards as well as Cabet, were to leave in the following September.

But the revolution of February 24, 1848, came suddenly, overthrowing all plans and destroying all their means.

REVOLUTION OF FEBRUARY 24, 1848.

The Icarians everywhere and at all times proved themselves courageous and devoted. Everywhere they were applauded for their brave, generous, disinterested conduct.

Upon the twenty-fifth Cabet had posted upon all the walls of Paris a proclamation, since become celebrated, in which he urged all to unite in support of the provisional Government; to act with moderation and generosity (no vengeance, no striking at property); to postpone the carrying out of the Icarian system and to act only as Frenchmen, Patriots, Democrats and Republicans. It has been admitted since that perhaps greater service had never been rendered by the Society.

But many Icarians hoping for progress in France as the result of the Revolution, no longer wished to emigrate;

many others were ruined and could neither leave nor make such a sacrifice as was required, while persecution everywhere paralyzed all.

NEW PERSECUTION.

It is horrible! The men of the *National* and of the *Reform* Parties, for a long time the enemies of the Icarians because they were peaceful, had secured control of the provisional Government, and found themselves yet the enemies of the Communists either through rancor and vengeance or because they wished a *bourgeoisie* Republic, while the Icarians demanded a *popular* or *democratic* Republic.

During the first days of the Revolution they adopted against the Icarians, not alone in Paris, but in all France, an extensive *system* of *slander* and *persecution* in order to exclude them from elections and employment, from the national guard and the national Assembly. The Communists were treated as Pariahs or outlaws. On April 16th the Government published or permitted to be published, through the Reactionary army, the propaganda —*"Down with the Communists, Death to Cabet."* The awful events of the 15th of May and the 23rd of June were perfidiously attributed to the Communists; the direction of all the movements was imputed falsely and traitorously to Cabet; warrants were issued against him; he was continually threatened with assassination and forced to remain in hiding.

However, in spite of these frightful difficulties, two other Advance Guards and four large convoys of families, about five hundred Icarians in all, left for Texas in 1848. The 2nd Advance Guard then rejoined the 1st.

But these Advance Guards upon arriving at New Orleans, met there the first two Advance Guards who were returning from Texas.

THE RETURN OF THE FIRST TWO ADVANCE GUARDS.

The first Advance Guard carried away by Cabet's enthusiasm and fervency neglected his warnings and advice and exposed themselves too much to fatigue and the hot sun of this region. These first Communists deprived of news from France, frightened by the disasters of April, May and June, by false and sinister rumors and especially that of the death of Cabet by assassination, and demoralized by a fever which claimed some victims, unfortunately abandoned Texas and returned to New Orleans with the second Advance Guard at a time when the others were arriving in their turn from France.

The disheartening news of this deplorable retreat which all preceding advices prevented foreseeing, came, like a thunderbolt, to strike Cabet at the moment when he was being persecuted before a court which condemned him to a month's imprisonment because, in May, 1848, some guns had been found in the office of the *Populaire*. However, he left immediately and not without difficulty, declaring from or at Boulogne, that he would return for the purpose of giving himself up.

DEPARTURE OF CABET.

He left Paris on December 13, 1848, during the winter, since London, Liverpool, New York and New Orleans were being ravaged by the Cholera, arriving at the latter city on January 19, 1849.

Upon his arrival he called a general Assembly and demanded a full explanation. He proposed to abandon the enterprise if such was the unanimous wish or to continue it with those who were determined, by giving two hundred francs to each of those who wished to withdraw.

The majority, 280 (142 men, 74 women, and 64 children) remaining steadfast, about twenty thousand francs was collected to repay those who wished to withdraw, and on March

All enter and leave the workshops at the same time.

Breakfast, dinner and supper are eaten in common.

Women who are about to be confined or are nursing children may be authorized to work at their homes.

There is equality in meals as elsewhere.

The Managers are the servants of all their brothers.

After supper come the recreations, good times, meetings, courts, General Assembly, discussions.

On Sunday there is instruction in True Christianity, admission of new members, marriages, individual or common promenading with music and country-like meals, good times, a concert and the evening play.

The Colony has a *Constitution,* of 183 articles, deliberated upon during nine meetings and finally accepted unanimously. There was debated and voted upon also during many meetings a law in regard to the General Assembly and one regarding admission to, withdrawal and exclusion from Icarian membership.

The Colony has obtained from the Illinois Legislature an act which incorporates and recognizes the *Icarian Community.*

Twice, unanimously, Cabet has been elected President of the Community and was reëlected a third time in 1852 during his absence, and three times since.

A fire which destroyed one of the barns, a flood that partially destroyed the mill, a storm that blew down the temple walls when their rebuilding had just begun caused some great losses. But a refectory for 800 persons has been built, together with its accompanying kitchen. The construction of a school has also been begun, etc., etc.

Some of the natives (whose commercial interests or prejudices have been offended) show the Colony little goodwill, but the people in general have shown it much sympathy since its arrival. They associate with the Icarians either in celebrating the anniversary of American independence, or in admitting them into their good times, their banquets, concerts, shows and balls.

Some have died or withdrawn, but there have been marriages (even with daughters of the country), births and recruits. The Icarian Colony today comprises 500 individuals, men, women and children; and but for the Revolution of 1848 it would certainly have been from 10 to 20,000.

But persecution has not been abandoned; it has pursued it from France to America; and in order to destroy the Colony, the Community and Communism, it attempts to morally kill its President and Counsellor.

SUIT AGAINST CABET IN PARIS.

We do not fear to state that no one, perhaps, has shown more *devotion* to the cause of the People and of Humanity since 1830 than has Cabet, especially since he left his family in December, 1848, in mid-winter, aged and suffering, to go to the assistance of his brothers 3000 leagues away, braving cholera and the formidable consequences of a first disaster.

No one perhaps has been more slandered and persecuted since 1830, precisely because of his devotion to the People.

We have already spoken of the cries for his death (a shameful thing for France) incited publicly against him on the 16th of April, by the national guard or Reactionaries. A short time before the Revolution of February, he was arrested, at the time of his return from England, and accused either of a conspiracy to dethrone Louis Philippe and take his place or of swindling under the pretext of asking money for the Icarians with the intention of leading them to Icaria. This second accusation so inconsistent with the first, was met by a multitude of protestations from the press and especially from the Icarians and was so absurd that it was unanimously put out of existence by the court of St. Quentin and even abandoned by the public ministry.

But Cabet had no sooner left, in December, 1848, than all the reactionary newspapers, profiting by his remoteness, leagued to overwhelm him with slander and insults.

Forced by the Reactionists, the government began a new prosecution accusing him of swindling, under the pretext that his colony was only a *fictitious, false, imaginary* enterprise for swindling the Icarians, and that his *Journey in Icaria,* his *True Christianity,* his *Populaire,* and his 40 or 50 other pamphlets, had been written and published after ten years of preparation for the purpose of perfecting the swindle. Nothing could be more evidently absurd and monstrous!

Moreover, as soon as the accusation became known, protests broke out from all sides, either from Icarians or from the Colony, or from the accused who demanded time to return from America to France in order to defend himself.

But the true condition of the Icarians was not known to the court nor to the magistrate charged with upholding the accusation and who was going to deny the existence of the Colony at Nauvoo; even to denying the existence of Nauvoo. The correctional court of Paris granted only insufficient delays; it judged Cabet in his absence, declared him guilty under the false pretext that he had no land in Texas, and condemned him to two years imprisonment and the deprivation of his political rights; which thing would prevent his election as deputy.

All the reactionary newspapers in France, even their accomplices in Germany, England and America, published the condemnation as a triumph: "There" said one of them, "is the man who was on the point of making himself dictator in March and April, 1848, condemned as a swindler!"

But hundreds of petitions signed by thousands of Icarians and Democrats in France, England, America, and especially in the Colony, came protesting against the monstrous iniquity of this condemnation, as disgraceful for France as the cries of *death to Cabet* uttered by the National Guard on April 16th under the eyes of the Provisional Government.

The electors of Paris protested also by choosing Cabet as their candidate, while he was absent, in all the later elections.

He protested himself either by writing several public letters to Louis Napoleon, to lodge a complaint, or to the President of the court for not forbidding judgment by default; or appealing to the higher court while making the return trip from America to France for the purpose of appearing before it, as soon as the progress of the Colony would permit him to leave it without danger to it.

RETURN OF CABET TO FRANCE.—HIS TRIUMPH.

Finally on May 15, 1851, he left the Colony for London and Paris, where he arrived after a journey of 3000 leagues by steamboats and railroads during a space of 23 days.

Nearly all his friends in England as well as in America opposed his going, convinced, they said, that it was a political scheme to kill the Colony and Communism or to prevent his election, and that in consequence he was doubtless condemned in advance.

But he persisted, convinced that it would be impossible to condemn him after hearing himself, convinced moreover that his *duty* was to brave the danger of the condemnation, resigned to all, even to martyrdom, and persuaded that the Colony was well enough organized, united enough, courageous and strong enough, to support itself in his absence and even during his imprisonment.

Arrived at Paris, he first gave himself up as a prisoner, for a month; then he appeared before the Court carrying the act by which the Peters Company had ceded to him a million acres of land in Texas.

Among other things, he said and demonstrated to the

Court that, if he had been ambitious and covetous, he would easily have secured all — power, honor and fortune; at first with Louis Philippe; then with Louis Napoleon whom he had known during their common exile in London, in 1838; then with the Provisional Government in 1848; that if, in place of making his proclamation of February 25th to excite the people to moderation and generosity, he had wished to enter into the Provisional Government, he would have done so, and that, in all later events, in March, April, May, his name would always have been written, unknown to him, among the members of a new Government or as a Dictator.

He also made known to the Court some of the leading principles of his Icarian system and doctrine, rapidly relating what he had done in Icaria and proved that no teaching was more moral, pure, more impressed with Humanity and Brotherhood, Equality and Liberty, justice and order, disinterestedness and devotion.

More than once he brought tears to the eyes of his judges; and the public ministry itself was constrained to present him a solemn vote of thanks in the name of society, for the great service he had rendered by his proclamation of the 25th of February.

Finally, after four days of discussion and a defense of four hours presented by the accused himself, in the presence of a large audience, the Court, after hearing all parties, annulled the condemnation through default.

And not one of the newspapers previously opposed to Cabet could forbear confessing that he came out of the combat with all the honors of victory.

And if the Icarians had been free to manifest their feelings by banquets, either in Paris or in the Departments, hundreds of thousands of Communists, Socialists and simple Democrats would have celebrated the victory of their Icarian leader as their common triumph.

PROSCRIPTION OF CABET AFTER THE SECOND OF DECEMBER.

But while Cabet prepared to return to Icaria, there suddenly blazed out the coup d'état of the 2nd of December. He was forced to hide during more than a month; finally, he was arrested at his home on January 26th, imprisoned in a casemate of Fort Bicêtre; then taken from his prison to be immediately transported by force to England on February 1st, as the *leader of the socialistic school* and as a *political agitator.*

THE ICARIAN COMMUNE IN FRANCE, OR IN ENGLAND.

An Icarian Commune in France would be very much easier than one in America, because one would avoid: the inconvenience, the fatigues and the enormous expense of transportation upon sea and land for 3000 leagues; the disorders of acclimatization; the difficulties of a strange language; the necessity of constructing everything, of establishing everything in the wilderness; the difficulty of finding, even of purchasing, many machines and things they would need; the difficulty of putting out and selling their products; the difficulty of procuring all scientific and other aids of civilization; the difficulty and slowness of correspondence, etc., etc.

The establishment of a Commune in England would have as many advantages and would be as easy as in France.

It would be even easier, since there is more liberty and independence; more money and greater fortunes; more chances to find the needed loan for such an enterprise.

But there was nothing to hope for in France at this time.

Cabet would have tried it in England, taking all necessary precautions, if he had been able to remain three or four months longer in 1852 to prepare the enterprise; for the ideas of Progress, Reform and Socialism are like generous and human sentiments, more common than one generally believes.

He would not doubt the complete success of an Icarian Commune in England, since the three years experience of the Icarian Colony at Nauvoo gave him the conviction that the Community is completely realizable with Icarians and money; and the complete success of a simple Icarian Commune in England, would determine the success of an Icarian State in America.

RETURN OF CABET TO ICARIA.

But Cabet could remain no longer in London; his duty called him to the Icarian Colony in America; he left for the New World in June, 1852, to realize there his first project of a Community in the wilderness.

THE ICARIAN COMMUNE IN AMERICA.— ESTABLISHMENT IN THE WILDERNESS.

In 1853, the Icarian Colony, provisionally established at Nauvoo, again took up its forward march into the wilderness. They decided that they would establish themselves in the south-western part of the State of Iowa, where they sent a first advance guard who took possession of the free lands bordering the Nodaway river. Since, we have purchased there nearly 4000 acres, and we are going to have at the end of the summer of 1855, a hundred people settled and nearly one hundred and fifty head of cattle, some hogs, some poultry, etc.

STATION AT NAUVOO.

Nauvoo will be maintained as a point of debarkation on the Mississippi, as a place for acclimating, as a place of apprenticeship and probation where emigrants will be received provisionally for trying the commune life; and from which after their definite admission, they will leave for the Icarian Commune.

We will now cast a rapid glance at the Icarian system or doctrine.

CHAPTER II.

A GENERAL IDEA OF THE ICARIAN SYSTEM.

DOCTRINE OR PRINCIPLE.

NATURE.— GOD.— We, Icarian Communists, do not believe that the Universe was the effect of *chance,* and we do like to admit a *first cause* absolutely intelligent and provident, that is called a *Creator, Supreme Being, God, Nature, Providence.*

We believe it to be useless and dangerous to insist upon discovering the origin, form, and essence of this first Cause; *useless* because we are convinced that it is the one *mystery* and human intelligence has not the understanding, or the means, or the necessary faculties to penetrate this mystery; *dangerous* because the examination of these questions leads to discussions which degenerate nearly always into disputes, divisions and even hatreds.

GOD, PERFECTION.— But we consider *God* as the *pre-eminent* and *all-powerful* One, as the *Infinite* and *Perfection* in all.

GOD, FATHER OF THE HUMAN RACE.— We like to consider God as the *Father* of the Human Race, as *love, goodness, justice, indulgence;* we imagine that he is the most perfect Father, the most just, the most tender; that this better Father has only love for his children and that he loves them all equally.

DESTINY OF HUMANITY; HAPPINESS.— We like to admit that God, the most perfect of Fathers, has willed *happiness* for his children on earth. We see that he has lavished all (air, warmth, light, water, earth, with its metals, fruits, and animals) to make us happy in satisfying all our needs (food, lodging, dress, protection, etc., etc.); and we believe that the *instinct, intelligence* and *reason* that he has given us, suffice with his other gifts, to assure the happiness of mankind.

EVIL, MISFORTUNE.— However, the history of all Peoples, in all times, shows us *evil* everywhere; the *wretchedness* of the mass by the side of the opulence of a small minority; *vices* and *crimes* born from opulence as from misery; ignorance and oppression; the exploitation of the Poor by the Rich; the desperation and insurrections of the Poor threatening continually the Rich and troubling their security; murders and criminal punishments; revolutions and reactions ceaselessly leading to new despair, new insurrections, and new calamities. In a word we see Man unfortunate nearly everywhere and always.

But we cannot believe that this must be the destiny of Humanity; we cannot believe that the *evil* must be without *remedy;* for Man is essentially sociable, intelligent and perfectible.

SOCIABILITY, GOOD NATURE.— Man is *sociable* and consequently attracted toward his like, sympathetic, compassionate, affectionate, naturally good.

INTELLIGENCE.— Man is eminently intelligent.

PERFECTIBILITY.— Man is evidently perfectible through experience and education.

But what is the *remedy* for the evil? and first, what is the cause?

CAUSE OF EVIL.— We believe that the cause is in a *bad social* and *political organization,* resulting from the ignorance, inexperience and error of Humankind from its beginning.

REMEDY.— We believe that the remedy must be in a *better social* and *political organization.*

THE BASIS OF A BETTER SOCIAL ORGANIZATION.

We believe that this better social organization must have for its basis principles contrary to those which are the cause of evil; that is to say, *Brotherhood, Equality, Solidarity;* the suppression of poverty and individual property, in a word *Communism.* For us, the remedy is in the fraternal and politically equal association that we call the *Community.*

THE COMMUNITY.— The Community is a great association or a great universal society, partnership or company, organized and based upon the principle of human *Fraternity* with all its consequences, in which the associates consent to put in common all their goods, abilities and work, to produce and enjoy in common.

SOCIETY.— It is a true Society in which there are not any exploiters and exploited, but true associates, all brothers and equals.

It is an *organized* company which must show organization and order everywhere, with intelligence and reason as well.

FRATERNITY.— Fraternity is for us the essential, radical or fundamental principle, generator of all other principles, and which necessarily comprehends all in itself alone.

Fraternity is itself the consequence of the other principle stated at the beginning, that the Supreme Being or God is the Father of all men; from which it follows that all men are his children, that all are brothers, and that the Human Race forms only one family of which all the members should love one another and devote themselves mutually to their interest and common welfare, as we conceive that they should be the most perfect brothers.

For us, the consequences of Fraternity are Solidarity, Unity, Equality, Liberty, the suppression of individual property and money, the improvement of Education, the purification of marriage and the family and the organization of work.

The principle of *Fraternity* is a principle at once philosophical and religious, social and political.

In our eyes, it is the most advanced and fruitful idea; it is the principle of the Evangels and Christianity. In a way we believe we can say, from the present, that our Icarian Communism is the purest morality, the sweetest philosophy and the most sublime religion, since it is nothing else than *Christianity* in its primitive purity, such as Jesus Christ instituted.

ICARIAN COMMUNISM IS THE TRUE CHRISTIANITY.

Christ came to bring a *new law,* a new social principle, a new system of organization for society, which he called the *Reign or the Kingdom of God, the new City.*

To Him, God was the *soul, love, life, Father* of Humanity. He spoke of Himself sometimes as the *Son of God,* sometimes as the *Son of Man, Brother* of other men, especially of the Poor, the Oppressed and the Unfortunate. He repeated without ceasing that all men are sons of God and brothers.

He contented Himself with two general and leading principles or commandments; the first, *love God* (which is the spirit, love, life, justice, happiness, all-powerful, infinite, perfection in all, etc.), and the second, *love your neighbor or your brother as your self;* and he added that these two commandments blended themselves in the making of one only, this being *all the law and the prophets.* His great social principle then was *Fraternity* of men and people. He said: love in order to be loved, help in order to be helped. He adopted these philosophical maxims: "Do not to another that which you would not wish that he do to you; do to others that which you would wish that they would do to you."

As secondary principles, he proclaimed Association, Equality, Liberty, Unity, Progress and indefinite Perfection.

He especially combatted MISERY; and, to suppress it, he recommended *Community* of goods, declaring that wealth prevented one from entering into the Kingdom of God.

The Apostles, the fathers of the church, and the early Christians employed the Community system; and if, in place of establishing Communities of men alone or of women alone, they had established Communities of men and women with the institution of marriage and the family, Communities for agriculture and trade, Community life would to-day be established throughout the whole world.

Since that time the Barbarians have invaded the Christian empire, and have established individual property of land and of men through the conquest; but bondage or slavery and feudal property have ceased; progress has marched with Revolution and reforms; the bourgeoisie has emancipated itself; Communes have been formed or enfranchised; Communities and corporations have been organized everywhere; the proletarian has gained his liberty; the French Revolution has proclaimed a new Fraternity, Equality and Liberty; all this has been accomplished through the influence of the Gospel and Christianity; and we Icarian Communists devote ourselves to the continuance of this progress by continuing to realize the teaching of Jesus Christ.

THE ICARIANS ARE TRUE CHRISTIANS.— Our Icarian Communism is then the true Christianity; we are *true Christians* — the disciples of Jesus Christ; it is His Gospel which is our Code, and it is His teaching which is our guide.

DEMOCRACY, REPUBLIC.— As we wish that His fundamental principle, *Fraternity,* with its consequences, Equality and Liberty, may be the source and soul of all the laws, institutions and customs in the Community, we can say also that Communism such as ours is the realization of Democracy and the Republic.

To close these first general ideas, some words on *poverty* and the establishment of the Community through the *voluntary and free consent* of the individual will be added.

POVERTY.— All Antiquity, even before Jesus Christ, cried out continually against the *misery* of the mass and the opulence of the few, which necessarily produces this misery.

The extinction of poverty was the most habitual object of the solicitude of Jesus Christ, who, in order to suppress it, established Community of goods.

The Fathers of the Church wished, through His example, to suppress poverty by establishing Communism. St. John Chrysostos, patriarch or pope of Constantinople, said:

> "It is less horrible to be murdered by a madman, than to be tormented by poverty; a bite is not lasting and heals; while poverty more cruel than a ferocious beast and more ardent than a furnace, bruises and destroys you without relaxing."

ESTABLISHMENT OF THE COMMUNITY THROUGH FREE AND VOLUNTARY CONSENT.— But Jesus Christ, His Apostles, the Fathers of the Church, and even Philosophers did not demand, in establishing Communism, spoliation through force or division of land by a suit at agrarian law, but the free and voluntary consent of the proprietors. We Icarian Communists demand the same consent, the same willingness, the same liberty.

Yet again, our Icarian Communism is no other thing than Christianity in its primitive purity.

CHAPTER III.

ICARIAN SOCIAL ORGANIZATION.

In the Icarian system, the Colony, the State, or the Nation, forms a true Society.

This Society is perfectly free and voluntary, that is to say, it imposes itself on no one, and it does not force (can not force) any one to enter; it includes only those who, voluntarily, freely, in perfect knowledge of motive, consent to become a part; and it admits only those who understand well, and who adopt completely its principles and conditions, and who unite the necessary qualities.

This Society makes its own social contract or constitution and its laws.

It determines its own social and political organization, institutes its public functions and chooses its functionaries.

It takes all means of preventing wretchedness and poverty, ignorance or superstition, and of assuring well-being and abundance, Education, Equality, Order and Liberty.

Its organization has for its *fundamental* and *generative principle, Fraternity.*

And once for all, it can be said and repeated that it is the purest Morals, the sweetest Philosophy and most sublime Religion.

It is also a *Society* of *mutual help,* a *universal assurance,* a true family, the members of which call themselves brothers, engaging themselves to practice the principles of the Brotherhood.

There each works *for all,* and all work *for each.*

It has for secondary principles, Equality, Solidarity, Community and Unity, which are the necessary consequences of Fraternity.

It is a blending of Communism and individualism; the home, for example, is individual, each having a home for himself, wife and family; but the property, in place of being individual or personal, is social, undivided, and common or public or national.

Profoundly convinced by experience that one can have happiness only through *fraternal association* and *Equality,* the Icarians wished to form a *Society* founded on the basis of the most complete and perfect *Equality.* All must be *Associates, Citizens, Equals in rights and duties,* without any sort of privilege for any one; all must partake equally in the *expenses* of the association, each following his *necessity* and the *advantages* of the Society, and his own needs.

All must form only one family, of which all members are united by the ties of Brotherhood.

All must form a *People* or a *Nation* of brothers; all laws must have for their purpose the establishing of *Equality* between them in all cases in which this equality is not practically impossible.

Even then all form only one Society, one family, one People. The land-holdings with all their subterranean riches, productions and superior constructions, form only one *domain,* which is *social* or *national.* This socialization facilitates immense economies and perfection in exploitation, which in turn assures an indefinite augmentation in production, abundance and well-being.

All movable goods of the members, with all the products of the soil, of agriculture and of industry, form only ONE CAPITAL which, like the landed holdings, is *social* or *national,* puts a great power at the disposition of the Society, and gives it the means of producing abundantly for all.

Thus, doing for the association alone, the putting of all in common, has innumerable advantages which no other social system can procure.

Communism renders the administration of the Society and the agricultural and industrial exploitation extremely easy and productive, through realizing enormous savings, prodigiously augmenting production, and creating abundance and well-being for all without exception.

This estate and capital belong undivided to the People, who cultivate and exploit them in common, administer them for themselves or their proxies, and distribute equally all agricultural and industrial products.

All Icarians are Partners and Equals, all must work, and as they have like interests all exercise their intelligence in finding the means, and especially the machines, which render their work easy and short, without dislike, fatigue and danger, and even agreeable and attractive.

The implements and the materials for work are furnished

from the social capital, as all products of agriculture and industry are gathered and placed in the public stores.

All members are fed, dressed, housed and furnished by means of the social capital; all are equally well provided for according to sex, age, etc.; and all take a like interest in successively adopting all possible improvements.

Thus, it is the Society (or the Family or the People) which alone is proprietor of all; distributes and organizes its work and its workers; constructs its workshops and stores; and procures its tools and raw materials. It is the Society also that cultivates the soil; constructs the houses, etc.; makes all the needed materials for food, dress, housing and furnishing, and finally feeds, dresses, houses and furnishes each family and each citizen. The Society admits only the necessary or useful industries, while setting aside the injurious or merely useless ones; it has everything made in quantity, in the great factories, for all members.

The Icarian Society founded on labor has also for its basis *order* and *organization* above all.

It is again founded on *Education*, on *Marriage* and the *Family.*

Education is considered as the base and center of the Society. The Icarian Republic agrees to educate all its children equally, similarly as it furnishes food equally to all. All children, girls as well as boys, receive the same general and elementary instruction, while each receives outside professional instruction suitable to the profession he chooses. All this instruction has for its purpose the fashioning of excellent workers, useful scholars, excellent parents and citizens, as well as true men.

Since *marriage* and the *family* are the chief condition of happiness for men, for women especially, and for children, the social organization is so prepared that all Icarians may be able to marry and have families. It is for this reason that the dower is abolished, that young women receive the same education as young men, and that the Republic assumes the responsibility of providing food, etc., and educating the children.

All precautions are taken to see that marriage assures the happiness of the husband and wife. However, if the common life becomes unbearable to one of them, divorce is permitted; but everything is so looked after as to make this remedy useless.

All Icarians can marry without opposition to their marriage, for the general rule is that all must do it, because marriage and the family are the best guarantee of order and peace in society, as of happiness for men, for women, and for children.

In the Icarian Republic *women* have the same social rights as men. The Icarians as a whole consider it their first duty and interest to assure the happiness of women.

It is equally the interest and duty of all Icarians, men and women, to protect all *children,* care for all *sick* and *infirm,* while being kind and respectful to all *old people.*

The whole social organization is so established as to suppress as much as possible the causes for *illness* (principally poverty, weakening or dangerous work and dissipation), to fortify the health and *improve* indefinitely the human species.

Hygiene is employed preferably to medicine.

The physician, etc., is a public officer or worker, interested in the advancement of the public health.

One of the principal regulations of the Icarian System is that it is necessary in everything to look first for the *necessity* of a thing, its utility, and for its *agreeableness* only in the last place. But it is the rule also that one must look for unlimited desirableness without other bounds than reason and equality in the enjoyment it may afford for all.

The Icarian System recognizes the *fine arts,* continuous *progress,* and the perpetual tendency toward perfection in all.

Religious opinions will be free and tolerated in Icaria, as likewise opinions on all other matters.

However, the Icarians have adopted the *True Christianity,* in its primitive purity, with its principles of Fraternity, Equality, Liberty, Partnership and Communism.

As for outward and public *worship,* it will be simple, without images, devoid of all ceremony and superstitious practices, principally devoted to the admiration of the Universe, thankfulness toward the Supreme Being, instruction on the social duties and the practice of Fraternity.

There will be no clergy forming a sacerdotal body.

We can even repeat that our Icarian Communism is none other than Christianity such as Jesus Christ instituted.

We repeat it, Icarians are *true Christians,* disciples, imitators and workers of Jesus Christ, applying His Gospel and Teachings while working to realize His Kingdom of God, His new City, and His Paradise on earth.

ADVANTAGES OF THE ICARIAN COMMUNITY.

We repeat it also, our Community is perfectly voluntary. Our whole Icarian System places in common the land and all capital, the development of intelligence and activity through instruction and education, the abolition of useless work, employing all capacities and all arms, and the organization of the work. Machines are multiplied to infinity, thereby realizing such great economies and so much increasing agricultural and industrial production that *abundance* and *well-being* are assured for all, while removing at once poverty and wealth which are the source of nearly all disorders.

In its turn well-being, united with Fraternity, Education, work and the suppression of celibacy, must generally strike the root of all vices and crimes.

Chapter IV.

Political Organization of Icaria.

OF THE COMMUNITY.

Since the Icarians are all brothers, partners and equal in rights, they are all members of the Popular Assembly; they all take part equally in debate, in the regulation and administration of their common or public affairs.

All are members of the People and of the public force or the civic or national guard and of the Jury.

They do, themselves and directly, all that they can, therefore, they name proxies or officers only when it becomes necessary.

All officers are elected and hold their positions in the interest of the People; all are proxies and servants; all are elective, temporary, responsible and revocable.

The government is a radical and pure *Democracy.*

It is a democratic *Republic.*

It is based not alone on Fraternity and Equality, but also on the Sovereignty of the People, on universal Suffrage, on Liberty and respect for laws.

The State is not a monarchy, neither is it a dynasty, an oligarchy, nor an aristocracy; it is the People.

The People are Sovereign, to them belongs the right of making or accepting and revising the Community's social organization, constitution and laws.

The State regulates all that concerns an individual, his actions, goods, food, dress, house, education, work, and even pleasures.

Each citizen exercises his portion of sovereignty through his vote and right of initiative or of proposing, and through his right of electorship and eligibility to office.

In order that the right of initiative and proposal may be exercised most effectively and usefully, the People are divided into small committees or groups among whom are distributed all the different branches of public affairs, in such a manner that each group occupies itself more specially with proposals having to do with the kind of question especially confided to that group.

All is so disposed that each individual can easily and freely exercise all his rights.

All is equally disposed so that each group may be perfectly independent of others, and thus can exercise its rights in perfect understanding of the case.

A newspaper, managed by the officers and distributed gratuitously to all citizens, makes known to all the facts which interest them and of which their knowledge is necessary.

As long as the People can come together in a single Assembly they will continue to exercise directly the legislative power. When the number becomes so great that it is practically impossible thus to assemble, the power to prepare or draw up drafts of laws will be delegated to deputies elected by them, who shall be temporary, responsible, and subject to recall. The right of accepting or rejecting proposals thus drawn is reserved to the head Popular Assembly.

In all cases, the executive power, charged with executing the laws, is essentially subordinated to the legislative and without power to restrain it.

Chapter V.

The Icarian Commune.

The Icarian *Commune* is the foundation of the Icarian *State* which is composed of many communes.

It is a little democratic *Republic.*

The population of the Commune must not exceed the number of citizens who can unite in a single Assembly, about 1,000 or 1,200, with their wives and children, about 4 or 5,000 souls.

Its *land-holdings* must be extensive enough: 1st, so that they will provide sites for the particular houses, workshops, stores and civic establishments or public buildings; 2nd, to provide agricultural lands necessary for the providing of food and other needs of the population.

The Icarian Commune was not constituted irregularly, by chance as it were, following the caprice of each member, but after a *general plan* carefully drawn, thoroughly discussed and finally adopted. This plan indicates in detail the squares, streets, houses, workshops, stores, public buildings, walks, etc., etc.

All buildings, special houses, workshops, stores, and public monuments will be constituted according to the *particular plans* previously discussed and adopted.

Each *house* will be built *for one family,* since everyone must marry. This house, simple at first, may become in the end as commodious, complete and agreeable as possible or needful according to the personal desires of the occupants. There shall be a little garden for verdure and flowers.

These houses have no workshops, implements, storehouses or stables in connection, since all work is done in the large common workshops, all products are put in the large public storehouses, and all horses are confined in one or several large common stables.

All workshops are *located* the most conveniently possible under all conditions, even that of ornament and point of view being duly considered.

The *unhealthful* and dirty workshops are located far from the dwelling-houses.

Everything is made in quantity for all citizens.

Each manufacture and each product is regulated by consumption, which in turn is determined by the necessary *statistics.*

The workers distribute themselves according to the need of each factory.

Each workshop *chooses* its manager.

There is a large bakery and also a large butchery, one or several large kitchens and dining rooms for the preparation and the serving of the common meals, and a large laundry with its wash-house and drying-room.

There is a school for all children, with its gymnasium; a museum; a hospital with its pharmacy and its baths for all the sick; a library; a printing-shop; one or several theaters; public games; a common house or city hall for popular assemblies, government, meetings, speeches, balls, concerts; a temple, etc., etc.

As soon as possible there will be one or several large *reservoirs* for distributing to all buildings light, heat and water, in such a manner that each family may have its particular *bath*. Each will also have its little *pharmacy,* furnished gratuitously through the large common pharmacy.

As soon as possible also the Commune will distribute to each family the little needful *provisions* for breakfast and for the evening collation. The main meal of the day, after work, must remain common according to the principles of fraternity, economy and advantage.

As soon as possible each workshop will have its *dressing-room* where will be placed the working garments which will be taken by the workers upon entering and put back when leaving so that the citizens may always be properly dressed outside the workshop.

The workshops and the storehouses will be located in the outskirts, the streets will be neither over-worked nor dirty, and their *paving* can be suited to the special conditions and as expensive as demanded.

In the Icarian Community, all land is communal, common or social, belonging undivided to all members of the Commune, and administered, exploited, cultivated and harvested, by all in common, and in the interest of all, in such a manner that all have equal freedom and well-being.

In order to realize all economies, all production and all abundance possible the land is considered as one *demesne.* This condition requires only one agricultural working, operated under the one plan only for the several crops, for gardening, for the fruits, for the woods, for the pastures and the large herds of necessary cattle, for the watering and the roads, for the distribution of the cultivators, for the workshops, machines, stores, and even for the charm of the landscape.

And as all members of the Commune are equally interested in perfection in agriculture, all discuss and decide together every question which concerns the land and agriculture as an industry.

One easily sees all the advantages which result from the Community; we have but indicated some of the principal ones.

And let us see what evil it suppresses.

Chapter VI.

Evil Abolished by the Community.

The simple fact of putting goods in common, the suppression of individual property, or of the existence of the Community, entails necessarily the suppression: of inheritances and divisions; of selling and buying; of money for internal affairs; of lending at interest and usury; of banking, crediting and discounting; of internal trade and shops; of debts, of bills of exchange and bills payable at sight; of the Exchange and stock-jobbing; of competition, monopolies and obstruction in trade; of failures; of division, lawsuits, seizures, arrests for debt; of civil courts and courts of commerce; of judges, counsellors, attorneys, solicitors, bailiffs, notaries, stock-brokers, etc.

The abolition of money, of selling and trade, adds to the well-being of all, bringing about, as it does, the abolition of robbery and fraud of all kinds and of nearly all other crimes; of criminal courts, prisons, and jails; of police and constables, etc.

The organization of work puts down strikes and rioting; workmen's certificates; distasteful, drawn out and dangerous work; excessive, useless, luxurious, and injurious manufactures; and idleness.

The doing away of useless work employs all hands, secures the perfection of professional training, the use of an infinite number of machines, together with organization and concentration, realizing so many economies and increasing so much production and abundance that they do away with *poverty* and wealth, pauperism, the proletariat, the beggar, and the vagabond. The condition so produced abolishes the need for all taxes (stamps, registering, town-dues, customs, passports, etc., etc.) other than work.

Marriage for all entails the suppression of disorders and scandals in families, of many crimes, of debauchery and prostitution.

There will be no more servants, salaries, lotteries, gambling and disorderly houses, revelling, and taverns.

With the abolition of the many bad things will come an immense and rapid uplifting of humankind.

Chapter VII.

The Excellence of the Community.

Thus, the Community is the most *complete* of all Socialistic Systems. It settles all questions, while nearly all other systems settle only a *few* and remedy only a part of the evil.

While the most complete it is also the *simplest* because it produces unity everywhere, notably in production, distribution and consumption.

It is again the *easiest* to realize, because it perfects all at the same time, conciliates all interests, ruins no one, guarantees the existence of all, and produces the greatest power for promoting the well-being of all.

The Society plainly contains already innumerable Communistic institutions; to completely organize the Community it is necessary to further increase the number. It is not even necessary that absolutely all may be in common; individualism should be especially conserved where it is preferable, in the home for example, in the same way that it is well, on all questions, to consult reason and utility in deciding what may be individual and what may be in common. The Community is then an Association of blended individualism and Communism, in which Communism dominates and in which notably, property is common.

The character of common property, social or national, is not in itself a novelty, for actual society knows already a very great number of national, communal or social properties belonging undivided to families or voluntary associations who place their goods in common, etc., etc. It suffices to increase rather than diminish the number of these common properties.

Chapter VIII.

The Icarian Constitution.— Laws.

Citizen Cabet, author of the *Journey in Icaria* and founder of the social and the political system of the Icarian Community, consented to make with all Icarians who will be received through him, an experiment of his system, and to expatriate himself for the purpose of trying an Icarian Colony in America, on condition that he would be during ten years, Manager or Director solely and absolutely for experiment, with power to direct it after his teachings and ideas, in order to unite the possible chances of success.

An obligation or contract was then freely and voluntarily entered into between him and the Icarians, and this contract, truly sacred, was executed in 1850 on the one hand by

Citizen Cabet, who has consecrated his life to Emigration and the Colony, and upon the other hand by the Icarians who have followed him to Nauvoo. All were well resolved to continue to execute it as long as it would not be modified by a convention mutually consenting.

Citizen Cabet would not have consented to any important modification if he had believed it useless or dangerous to the Colony and Community.

But he has believed a modification necessary in order to put the Social Contract in harmony with the law and the republican sentiment of the Americans. He has not seen any inconvenience, moreover, in profiting from the experience acquired in the year just past, in applying to the present the radical democratic principles which must always a little later govern the Community.

Consequently, Citizen Cabet himself proposed in January, 1850, to replace the only and absolute manager during ten years by a multiple managership, elective and annual, while submitting himself to re-election.

He has proposed to modify the first Social Contract and replace it by a Constitution.

This Constitution, proposed by him, discussed during eight meetings was voted unanimously on February 21, 1850. Then after the *Bill* of incorporation for the Icarian Community passed the Legislature of Illinois, it was revised, debated and voted upon anew with unanimity, on May 4, 1851, as follows:

ICARIAN CONSTITUTION.

Chapter I.

PRELIMINARY CONSIDERATIONS.

Nature has overwhelmed Man with kindness. She has poured out upon the earth, around Man, all the elements and productions necessary to teach him the use of these things. She has desired the happiness of Humanity above all things else. And still history shows us Man unhappy nearly everywhere and always.

Man is by nature sociable, consequently sympathetic, affectionate and good. Yet history shows us, in every time and all countries, vice and crime, oppression and tyranny, insurrections excited by despair, and civil wars, proscriptions and massacres, anguish and torture.

But Man is highly *perfectible;* consequently human *progress* is a natural law and evil can not be without remedy.

If evil had its origin in the vengeance of a jealous and pitiless God who imposed eternal punishment upon the innocent posterity of a sinful person, whose disobedience came through the temptation of an irresistible power, one must despair of a remedy and resign himself to suffer. But this vengeance and punishment is repugnant to all our ideas of justice, of kindness, of divine love and perfection; consequently we must look elsewhere for the true cause of evil.

This cause we find in a social *organization* resulting from inexperience, from ignorance and from the mistakes of Man in his infancy. Hence, we may find the remedy in a *better social organization* founded on a superior principle.

Let us replace the olden times by the new, the reign of Satan or of Evil, by the reign of God or of Good; spiritual Death by the Resurrection, Regeneration and Life; Darkness by Light; Routine and Prejudice by the Experience of the centuries; Error by Truth; Ignorance by Knowledge and Learning; Injustice by Justice; Domination and Servitude by Enfranchisement and Liberty.

Let us substitute the welfare of all for the excessive opulence of the privileged few who have nearly everything without working, and who are running over with abundance while the masses who work and produce have nearly nothing, lack the necessities, and suffer from the enslavement of misery.

Let us substitute for a Religion overburdened with superstition, intolerance and fanaticism, one that is reasonable and which teaches men to love and help each other.

May we adopt a social organization in which the word *Society* may not be a word of reproach and derision, but a truth and a reality, and in which there is neither antagonism nor competition, no exploitation of man by man, neither masters, servants, nor hirelings, proletariat nor pauperism, idleness nor excessive labor.

Let us replace individual property, the source of all abuse, by social property, common, undivided, which has none of the objections of the first and which is infinitely more productive for the use of all.

Let us purify and perfect Marriage and the Family through the suppression of dowries, through the education of women as well as men, and through liberty in the choice of a spouse.

In a word, the old Society is based on individualism. Give us, as a basis for the new, Fraternity, Equality and Liberty, Communism or the Community.

Chapter II.
GENERAL PRINCIPLES.

Section I.— Society.

Art. 1.— The Icarians form among themselves a true *Society.* They are all *Associates.*

Art. 2.— This Society includes all who are or will be definitely admitted, with their wives and children.

Art. 3.— It is established in the interest of its members, to guarantee, as much as possible, their natural rights and to assure their happiness.

Art. 4.— It is established also in the interest of all Humanity, through devotion to this one to present a form of Society capable of producing happiness and to prove, through experience, that Communism, based on Fraternity, is realizable and possible.

Art. 5.— It has for material end the clearing and cultivation of the soil, the construction of houses, the engaging in all useful industries; in a word, to make fertile and to civilize the wilderness.

Art. 6.— It is at once agricultural and industrial, civil and political.

Art. 7.— The number of its members is unlimited.

Art. 8.— It is destined to become a City and a State obedient to the general laws of the United States.

Art. 9.— In the meantime it is obedient to the laws of the State of Illinois.

Art. 10.— Aliens of all countries can readily adapt themselves to the Icarian Doctrine and meet all the conditions exacted for admission.

Art. 11.— The conditions and mode of admission are controlled by a specific law.

Art. 12.— Its Social Capital includes the fortunes of all the Associates. Each brings to the Society all that he possesses, without any exception.

Art. 13.— The Society is planned to be perpetual. However, an Associate may withdraw or may be expelled, as will be explained in the special regulation for admission, withdrawal and expulsion.

Art. 14.— The Constitution and Laws are made by the People and for the People.

Art. 15.— All powers come from the People and are established in their interest.

Art. 16.— The Government is that of a Democratic Republic.

Art. 17.— The Icarian Society is based on the principles of Fraternity and Communism.

Art. 18.— It has adopted the name of "The Icarian Community."

SECTION II.— FRATERNITY.

Art. 19.— Fraternity of Men and of Peoples is the fundamental and generative principle of the Icarian Community.

Art. 20.— All Icarians recognize or adopt each other as brothers.

Art. 21.— They say that their purpose is to love, aid, relieve and defend each other as brothers.

Art. 22.— This principle is identified with the evangelic precept: "*Love your neighbor as yourself,*" or with this philosophic precept: "*Do not to another that which you would not wish that he do to you; on the contrary, do to others that which you would wish they would do to you.*"

Art. 23.— This principle of Fraternity will be the soul of the Constitution and Laws, of the manners and customs.

Art. 24.— It must be inculcated through the training of the child, and applied everywhere with all its consequences.

Art. 25.— Its principal results are *Equality,* Liberty, Unity, Solidarity.

SECTION III.— EQUALITY.

Art. 26.— The Icarians proclaim natural *Equality,* social or civil and political, without any privilege. They recognize all to be equals in law and duty.

Art. 27.— All have the right of being equally well fed, dressed, housed, taught, nursed, treated in everything; as all have the duty of being equally devoted to the Community.

Art. 28.— Servitude is done away with.

Art. 29.— Equality is *relative* and *proportional.* Each has an equal right in the benefits of the Community, *according to his needs,* and each has the equal duty of bearing the burdens, *according to his abilities.*

Art. 30.— All have the same part in the Sovereignty, the same right in the making of the Constitution and Laws. All are equally electors and eligible for all the public functions, at the age fixed by law.

SECTION IV.— LIBERTY.

Art. 31.— Liberty is natural, social or civil, political.

§1 — Natural Liberty.

Art. 32.— By nature, Man is essentially free; violence and force cannot give any one the right of domination and of mastery.

Art. 33.— The defence against all attack, the resistance to all oppression, are natural rights.

Art. 34.— But all men are equally free, and, in consequence, the liberty of each is necessarily limited by the liberty of others. No one is free to harm the liberty of another.

Art. 35.— No one is free to violate an *agreement* freely made, an engagement freely contracted.

§2 — Social or Civil Liberty.

Art. 36.— The end of Society is to guarantee natural liberty by the protecting of all through force if need be.

Art. 37.— Law, the expression of the social will, determines and fixes the necessary limits of liberty. It has the right to *forbid* all that is injurious, and of *ordering* all that is useful.

Art. 38.— License and anarchy are not liberty; they are the enemies of liberty.

Art. 39.— When law is made by the People and for the People, it forbids only that which is injurious, and orders only that which is useful.

Art. 40.— Then, liberty is the right of doing that thing which is upheld by the law and of refraining from doing that which is not ordered by it.

Art. 41.— Obedience to the law is the exercise of liberty.

§3 — Political Liberty.

Art. 42.— This is the right of concurring directly or indirectly, as all others, in the exercise of Sovereignty and in the making of the Constitution and Laws.

SECTION V.— UNITY.

Art. 43.— Individualism has as many forms as there are individuals, the fractions and pieces are infinite, which produces weakness.

Art. 44.— Fraternity and Communism to the contrary lead to Concentration and Unity, which produces strength and power.

Art. 45.— The Icarian Community is founded on *Unity* in everything; in the people, who form only one family of brothers, and only one army of workers; in the territory which forms only one great domain; in agriculture, which forms only one vast exploitation of the soil; in industry, which forms only one vast industrial exploitation; in education, which forms only one great system of training for the entire People.

Art. 46.— Unity must be harmonized with all the *divisions* that indicate reason, science, the ease and usefulness of exploitation and work.

SECTION VI.— SOLIDARITY.

Art. 47.— Solidarity is also a consequence of Fraternity and Unity. All Icarians are jointly and separately liable the one toward the other for security and defence.

Art. 48.— The Icarian Community is a mutual and universal *assurance* against all accidents, disasters and misfortunes.

Art. 49.— Subscriptions and taxes are no longer necessary against fire, flood, strikes, sickness, ruin and misery.

Art. 50.— The Community provides each one with all he needs, the only condition being that he work according to his strength, while all accidents are prevented or suffered and repaired by it.

Art. 51.— There is no longer the proletariat, pauperism, begging or vagabondage in its midst.

SECTION VII.— RESPECT FOR LAW.

Art. 52.— The one principle of the Icarian Community is respect for law and submission of the minority to the majority.

Art. 53.— Before voting, each voter has the right of expressing, in all freedom, his opinion against the proposal in debate, but each voter tacitly agrees to submit himself to the future decision of the Assembly.

Art. 54.— The *Minority* must give way to the *Majority,* and carry out its decision without resistance, without complaint, without criticism, until the formal revision in the form laid down by the Constitution and Laws.

SECTION VIII.— COMMUNITY.

Art. 55.— Communism is the opposite of Individualism. Community in goods is the reverse of Individual Property.

CHAPTER III.

SOCIAL ORGANIZATION.

SECTION I — PROPERTY, CUSTOM.

Art. 56.— In the Icarian Community property is not individual, but social, common, undivided.

Art. 57.— Each Associate is a co-proprietor of all; but nothing is individual or personal, or the exclusive property of anyone: the Community alone is proprietor.

Art. 58.— Only, each can and must have the *use* or the pleasure of that which is needed, according to the rules established by law.

Art. 59.— The Community does away with these: 1, all *abuses* of property, *opulence* and *misery* that it engenders; 2, the right of *succession* and inheritance, by furnishing to all children and citizens what is needful for them; 3, *buying* and *selling, trafficking* and *bargaining,* with their *frauds* and *falsifications,* with their *cases* and their failures, by replacing them with the free distribution to all Associates of all things which they may need; 4, *money,* for internal use; 5, *banks* and *excessive interest rates;* 6, *wages* of workers; 7, the *pay* of public officers; 8, the *budget* and taxes; 9, *legal processes* and the *courts,* with their employees of all kinds.

SECTION II.— WAGES.

Art. 60.— All laborers are fed, housed, clothed, furnished with all, by the Community; consequently, wages are useless and are abolished.

SECTION III.— PUBLIC SALARIES.

Art. 61.— Public duties are labor, and the officers are fed, clothed, housed, etc.— as other workers; hence, salaries are useless and are abolished.

SECTION IV.— TAXES.

Art. 62.— Taxes of any kind are useless and have been abolished. There is no other tax than work, made short, easy, without fatigue and danger, even attractive, by means of instruction and unlimited machinery.

SECTION V.— ORGANIZATION OF WORK.

Art. 63.— Order and organization are necessary everywhere, principally in work.

Art. 64.— All the various industries are placed and combined in a manner to secure the greatest possible return.

Art. 65.— All work is done in the great common workshops conveniently located.

Art. 66.— Machines are provided without limit, to aid and ensure the worker, even to replacing him, in such a manner that man may one day be only a director of machines.

Art. 67.— Machines are materially useful in the Community, since they work for all without harming any one.

Art. 68.— All raw materials, tools, machines, are furnished by the Community, as all products are collected and distributed or employed by it.

Art. 69.— The workers form a peaceful army, directed by overseers chosen by themselves.

Art. 70.— Work is a public function.

Art. 71.— All kinds of work are equally esteemed and honored.

SECTION VI.— AGRICULTURE.

Art. 72.— All the above concerning industry, in general, applies to agricultural industry. The Community looks upon it as the basis of social wealth.

SECTION VII.— FOOD.

Art. 73.— The Community supplies its members with food.

Art. 74.— It regulates all things which concern food.

Art. 75.— It establishes, moreover, common meals.

Art. 76.— As soon as it can, it will provide some meals in each family, while furnishing to each all the needed provisions.

SECTION VIII.— HOUSING.

Art. 77.— The Community furnishes lodging for all members.

Art. 78.— As soon as it can it will provide a separate house for each family.

Art. 79.— It regulates all that concerns particular lodgings, all workshops, all public or common buildings, towns and villages.

SECTION IX.— CLOTHING.

Art. 80.— The Community clothes all its members; it regulates all that concerns dress.

Art. 81.— It harmonizes variety with unity and equality.

Section X.— Education.

Art. 82.— The Community provides an education for all its children.

Art. 83.— It places the children as it considers best, according to their particular interest and in the general interest; sets aside the part of their childhood and youth necessary to secure an education and regulates everything which may concern that.

Art. 84.— The education given is the most complete and perfect possible.

Art. 85.— The training is physical, moral, intellectual, professional, scientific, civic.

Art. 86.— The *physical* has for its end the making of robust and dextrous individuals.

Art. 87.— The *moral* training has as an end the forming of excellent citizens who practice the principle of *Brotherhood* and who are accomplished in all the duties of the social life.

Art. 88.— The *intellectual* education aims to develop to the highest point the intelligence of the Icarians, while giving to all the elements of all the sciences and arts.

Art. 89.— The *professional* purposes to train excellent artisans or workers for each trade and industry.

Art. 90.— The *scientific* training aims to produce Teachers and Scholars useful to Humanity.

Art. 91.— *Civic* training aims to make known the laws and the political and social duties.

Art. 92.— The elementary and general education is the same for men and women alike.

Art. 93.— Children of the same sex are cared for in separate schools.

Art. 94.— When the Community shall be completely established and developed, the children will be able to live with their parents while attending the schools for their common education.

SECTION XI.— MARRIAGE, FAMILY.

Art. 95.— The Community is based on marriage and the family, purified of all which alters or mars them.

Art. 96.— The voluntary celibate is interdicted; all those who can must marry.

Art. 97.— Law controls all that concerns marriage, family, paternal and maternal authority.

Art. 98.— Dowry is abolished.

Art. 99.— The choice of a spouse must be perfectly free.

Art. 100.— Husband and wife are equals, except for the precautions which will be imposed by the law in case of disagreement.

Art. 101.— The duty of faithfulness is the same for both.

Art. 102.— Marriage is contracted for life.

Art. 103.— Nevertheless, divorce will be authorized in the cases which are provided by law, and with the precautions which shall be prescribed.

Art. 104.— Each of the divorced parties will and must marry another.

SECTION XII.— DISEASE, THE FEEBLE.

Art. 105.— The education, hygiene, the general organization of the Society and of the work, must seek to diminish disease.

Art. 106.— The sick and infirm must be taken care of in a brotherly manner, whether in a public or common hospital or in their families as may be determined by the law or the common regulations.

Art. 107.— The physician, the surgeon, the pharmacist, the hospital attendant or nurse are workers who have their work and special place of work as do all other workers.

SECTION XIII.— WOMEN, CHILDREN, THE AGED.

Art. 108.— The Community guarantees: first, to women as a whole, from men as a whole, respect and regard; second, to the children, love; third, to the aged, regard and respect due them; fourth, to all, devotion and protection.

Section XIV.— Religion.

Art. 109.— The Icarian Community adopts Christianity in its primitive purity, with its fundamental principle, Brotherhood of Men and Peoples, as its Religion.

Chapter IV.

POLITICAL ORGANIZATION.

Section I.— Sovereignty.

Art. 110.— Sovereignty belongs to the Community.

Art. 111.—It is exercised concurrently in the name of the Community through the General Assembly and the Managership, each to the limits of its privileges.

Art. 112.— Each citizen exercises his portion of Sovereignty through his *vote.*

Art. 113.—Every vote is *public.* The written vote is *signed.*

Section II.— Public Powers.

Art. 114.— There are two great powers: the *legislative* and the *executive.*

Art. 115.— These two powers are necessarily distinct and separate.

Art. 116.— The executive is subordinate to the legislative.

Art. 117.— The legislative power is placed in a General Assembly, and the executive in a Board of Managers.

Art. 118.— The *judicial* power is exercised through the General Assembly or through a jury organized by law.

Section III.— The Legislative Power.

General Assembly.

Art. 119.— The Assembly is composed of all men who have been definitely admitted and who are twenty years of age.

Art. 120.— The women are admitted to a separate place, with consultative voice. They are expected to give their advice on all questions which particularly concern them.

Art. 121.— The General Assembly makes the Constitution and the Laws.

Art. 122.— The proposals for laws may be presented either by the Board of Managers or by the citizens.

Art. 123.— The procedure of the General Assembly is regulated by a special organic law.

Art. 124.— When the membership becomes too great, it will be replaced by the Popular Assemblies and by a representative or national Assembly, among which the legislative and judicial powers will be distributed by a special constitutional law.

SECTION IV.— EXECUTIVE POWER — BOARD OF MANAGERS.

§1.— Prerogatives of the Managers.

Art. 125.— The Managers are charged with the execution of the laws, and propose the necessary means for their execution.

Art. 126.— They are also charged with the administration conformably to the laws. They name all the officers or agents who are needed to aid them in this administration under their responsibility.

Art. 127.— Some laws are needed for authorizing borrowing and the purchase or sale of real estate.

Art. 128.— Special laws will provide for all commissions that will be needed from time to time.

§2.— Composition of Board of Managers.

Art. 129.— The Board is composed of six members.

Art. 130.— One of these shall be the President.

Art. 131.— These six members discuss and decide in common the principal questions.

Art. 132.— In case of disagreement, the President has the deciding voice.

Art. 133.— The Board can transact the business before it only when the members present or their assistants are not less than three in number.

Art. 134.— Each member of the Board may demand that his opinion be registered on every proposition arising and even be communicated to the General Assembly.

Art. 135.— Each member assumes the title of Member of the Board of Managers.

§3.— Election of the Board.

Art. 136.— The six members are elective.

Art. 137.— They are elected by the General Assembly.

Art. 138.— They are elected for a year.

Art. 139.— They are indefinitely reëligible.

Art. 140.— One-half are subject to reëlection every six months.

Art. 141.— They are elected by an absolute majority and by a written and signed ballot.

Art. 142.— The President shall be elected separately.

Art. 143.— The five remaining members of the Board shall be elected conjointly by ticket.

Art. 144.— Before election a list shall be drawn up on which will be placed all those who will be presented as candidates.

Art. 145.— Those to be voted for shall be taken only from the candidates whose names are so listed.

Art. 146.— Each candidate shall, in demanding that his name appear on the list, explain his motives as a candidate.

Art. 147.— The Assembly shall be consulted in case of dispute concerning the listing of any name. If ten members demand that the name be placed on the list, it shall be placed thereon.

Art. 148.— An open presentation of views shall be required of every candidate.

Art. 149.— The discussion shall be free and frank, but

dignified and brotherly, exclusively animated by the sentiment of general and common interest.

§4.— Division of Board Duties.

Art. 150.— The members of the Board divide the duties of administration among themselves.

Art. 151.— The duties are divided as follows:

1. The Presidency — Supervision and general direction;
2. General direction of finances and food;
3. General direction of housing and clothing;
4. General charge of education, of health and recreations;
5. General direction of industry and agriculture;
6. General direction of the secretaryship and of the printing-office.

Art. 152.— The members of the Board may not preside over the General Assembly.

§5 — The President.

Art. 153.— The President of the Board has the title of *President of the Icarian Community.*

Art. 154.— He represents the Community in all of its external relations.

Art. 155.— He acts, corresponds, negotiates, treats, appears in courts either as plaintiff or defendant, and signs all papers in his capacity as President of the Icarian Community.

§6 — Responsibility.

Art. 156.— The Board is responsible. At the beginning of each month it will present a summary of its work during the preceding month and of the financial situation as well. Every six months, eight days before the election, it shall render an account of its administration during the six months to the General Assembly and explain to it the situation of the Community.

§7.—*Public Duties.*

Art. 157.—All public duties are established in the interest of the Community.

Art. 158.—They are as numerous as necessary.

Art. 159.—All are a duty, an obligation, a work which one cannot give up without a legitimate excuse for so doing.

Art. 160.—The place where they exercise their duties is in the place of public office.

Art. 161.—The performance of their duties in the public office is mandatory.

Art. 162.—All offices are elective except as mentioned in Art. 126.

Art. 163.—Office is temporary, accountable and responsible.

Art. 164.—Each command shall be issued in a fraternal spirit and shall be obeyed with all due respect for the law.

Art. 165.—In case of abuse, either of the citizen by the officer or of the officer by the citizen, each has the right to protest or complain.

SECTION V.—JUDICIAL POWER.

§1.—*Offenses.*

Art. 166.—In the Community the offenses are: acts which wrong the Society or some of its members; violations of its principles, laws or regulations; the illegal disposition of a common object; want of care and economy; those things which would bring disorder and trouble into the great family.

Art. 167.—Falsehood and slander are inexcusable offenses.

Art. 168.—Insulting, criticising and speaking evil of the General Assembly are also offenses.

§2.—*Penalties.*

Art. 169.—The penalties are: 1st, censure in the workshop, or in the General Assembly, or in public with more or less of publicity; 2nd, exclusion from the workshop, or the General Assembly, or from the Community in those cases which may be determined by law.

§3.— *Reporting Offenses.*

Art. 170.— Each Workshop Director must report, in a weekly or special report, the offenses committed in his workshop.

Art. 171.— It is a duty of each citizen to make known, in the interest of the Community, the offenses committed against it.

Art. 172.— It is a duty of the Board of Managers to investigate offenses and demand against the offenders the execution of the laws.

§4.— *Judgment.*

Art. 173.— The offenses against workshop regulations are judged by the workshop.

Art. 174.— The common offenses against the Community are judged by the General Assembly or by a jury.

SECTION VI.— AMENDMENT.

Art. 175.— The Icarian People have necessarily the right to amend and modify the Constitution. But they can, in their interest, draw up rules and forms for the purpose of preventing the exposure of the Constitution to changes which are too precipitate or frequent.

Art. 176.— The Constitution may be revised only at two year intervals, in 1853, 1855, etc.

Art. 177.— The amending shall be done in March.

Art. 178.— Any one who may wish a complete or partial revision must ask it in writing, in the next to the last week of February.

Art. 179.— All others who would wish to modify or change it in any way must do it, in writing, in the same way and at the same time. These revisions must be posted during the last week of February.

Art. 180.— In the last week of March, the Assembly shall decide first by a majority of three-fourths, if it will consider the demand for amendment.

Art. 181.— In this case it shall fix the opening of the discussion for a day in the second week of March.

Art. 182.— Each member can propose, in writing, amendments to the changes proposed.

Art. 183.— The Assembly shall discuss and vote, by a majority of three-fourths, the total or partial revision of the Constitution.

Final Disposition.

A printed copy of the Constitution and principal laws, when the General Assembly shall so order, shall be sent to each member of the Community.

REGULATIONS FOR THE GENERAL ASSEMBLY.

A STATEMENT OF MOTIVES.

In every country, the law concerning the General Assembly is one of the most important, since it regulates the making of all other laws.

In Icaria especially, it is one of the fundamental laws and nearly constitutional.

The Icarian Constitution and the Icarian law of the General Assembly are perhaps the most liberal, the most democratic and the most popular that exist; for they declare and constitute the Sovereignty of the People, universal suffrage, the right of each citizen to propose laws, to discuss and vote upon them, while according to the *women* the right to assist in the Assemblies and to take part in all discussions, to express their minds and defend their interests.

The Icarian law goes the farthest; it declares that taking part in the General Assemblies is not alone a right, but a *duty*; and this principle, that participation is a duty, is a great step in the practice and organization of the Democracy.

It is a duty, in short, for the Icarian, either to himself or to his fellow-citizens, who are his brothers, or to the Community taken collectively.

It is a duty that he owes to himself, with respect to his proper interest and his personal dignity. An intelligent and rational being, jealous of the dignity of man, and trustworthy of the name of man in the highest acceptance of the word, must appreciate and desire the moral and intellectual pleasures before the material and sensual ones. He must wish Liberty, Equality and Fraternity above all, and do all things which will assure him the possession of these. He would merit neither the name of Democrat, nor even that of man, nor especially that of Icarian, who would disdain to exercise the rights of a citizen and, in consequence, to assist in the General Assemblies for the purpose of taking part in the making of the laws which must regulate his acts and his fate.

Also, especially the workers and the proletarians call for the recognition and the practice of the principle of the Sovereignty of the People, of universal suffrage and of the participation of each citizen in the making of the laws and the decisions on public affairs.

Now, if the Icarians could enjoy in Icaria all these advantages without any reserve and without any hindrance, would they not then be lacking and give themselves the lie if they should neglect to exercise their right?

Participation in the Assembly is also a duty for each Icarian toward his brothers, inasmuch as each owes to them the tribute of his intelligence, training, experience, ability, observations, opinions and counsels or advice. To be indifferent to the public welfare and the happiness of his brothers, to occupy himself only with his personal pleasures, would not only be an act of folly, which would compromise his particular interests, but would again be an act of selfishness of the bad citizen and bad brother.

Participation in the General Assembly is, again, a rigorous duty to the Community considered collectively, for the Community is profoundly interested in what improves its members and would raise them to a high moral plane as soon as possible, knowing all their interests, duties, laws, regulations, decisions, all that is needed to be done, is finally executed and put into practice. It is in the General Assembly alone that all learn, know and perfect themselves. One would necessarily harm the Community who, neglecting to take part in the Assemblies, would expose himself to the violation of the laws and the social obligations due to the error of not knowing them. This duty of taking part in the Assemblies, exists evidently for the one admitted provisionally as well as for those who are definitively admitted.

This duty evidently exists for the women as well as for the men, for the young girls and the young women as well as the older women, since the Community is quite evidently interested in seeing that they know what are their duties as well as their rights, all decisions and all regulations of conduct, to the end that they may be able to conform themselves to them.

The same may be said for the young men who are not in the schools.

The whole Colony must then be quite entirely united, as much as possible, in the General Assembly, for the purpose of drawing up and making the laws, while at the same time living together as brothers.

And anyone who, in place of taking part in the General Assembly, would go to pass the evening elsewhere, especially at the house of persons foreigners to the Community, would be equally lacking in his duties toward the Community.

It is the same when voting at an election. Abstinence would be unjustifiable, since it would be impossible for an Icarian not to know someone dignified and capable, either to be presented as a candidate or to be elected.

As for the form of voting, the public vote by "Yes" or "No" on the *call of the roll* is the most solemn, certain, democratic and Icarian. It must be employed always if it does not require too long a time, which can be better used. However, it will be agreed that it will be preferred for a vote on the whole of a law or for the important questions, or when the President of the Community shall demand it, or when ten members rise to ask for it.

And when in the voting at an election, as the necessity of an absolute majority would require several ballots and a great deal of time, one can see that the operation will be terminated necessarily at the third time of balloting, through a balloting between the two candidates who will have attained the most votes on the second ballot.

Since the election of the two Vice-Presidents and the three secretaries of the General Assembly would require too much time by written vote, it is reasonable to abridge and facilitate the operation by a rising vote.

The law of the thirtieth of January speaks of the *order of the day* being announced in advance of the discussion so that each person may prepare himself without being too much surprised. But in order to attain completely this end, it is necessary that the proposition to be discussed and its motives be drawn up in writing, read, published, posted, and then read in the Assembly. In order that the discussion may be complete, it is necessary that there must be, if some one demands it, a general discussion on the principle, then a discussion and a vote on each separate article, then finally, a general vote to adopt or reject the proposition.

It may serve a useful purpose to publish the important votes.

Must those Icarians who do not understand French perfectly be required to attend the Assemblies? There are some reasons for not requiring them to do so, but other reasons more numerous and stronger for refusing the exception. They would have a sort of an apparent privilege if they were excused; they would remain for a longer period strangers to the language; they would not undertake any part in the discussions or voting; they would be ignorant of nearly everything, would not be able to do anything, and would be as strangers in the midst of their brothers. But, if they are admitted without knowledge of the language and be obliged to take part in the Assemblies, it would be necessary to take all possible means to teach them the French and to make them understand the proposal, the discussion, the question to decide and the vote.

What is the number of votes necessary either for a deliberation or an election? The law of the thirtieth of January did not say, but we think that this number perhaps would be reasonably fixed at nine-tenths of the members present at the time and legally assigned and recognized.

Finally, six Commissioners, drawn by chance from the roll during a month, who will choose a chairman from among themselves, appeared necessary to verify those present and absent, those entering and those leaving, to do the placing, to count the votes, and generally to look after the order in the Assembly and make a report to the President of the Community.

Through these many considerations and wholly in keeping with the law of January 30, 1851, it is now proposed to the members of the Icarian Community to add the following regulations;

Art. 1.— It is an absolute duty for all Icarians, men and women, to participate in the General Assembly.

Art. 2.— An insurmountable difficulty alone should prevent it.

Art. 3.— Sickness, absence through public service, can alone be a legitimate excuse.

Art. 4.— Nurses of the sick even must participate as soon as they have been able to take the necessary measures for whatever thing may be required. Meanwhile, the Board of Managers will take the proper measures in order that they may know what has been done in the Assembly.

Art. 5.— The members who cannot speak French will not be exempted from participating in the Assembly, but the Board of Managers will take the necessary measures to make all known to them.

Art. 6.— Those who find it impossible to take part must, as soon as possible, notify the Bureau or the Board of Managers.

Art. 7.— Each must appear exactly at the hour indicated.

Art. 8.— The meeting must open regularly at the hour fixed.

Art. 9.— Women, provisionally admitted, young men, definitively admitted, are separately placed.

Art. 10.— Women have a special door for entering and leaving.

Art. 11.— Upon entering, each must take that place nearest the Bureau.

Art. 12.— No one must remain outside or on the steps.

Art. 13.— Each meeting will begin with the roll-call. Absences will be announced, approved or disapproved by the Assembly in the same meeting or at the following meeting.

Art. 14.— Nine-tenths of the members present in their places and not prohibited from voting are necessary to begin a discussion or election.

Art. 15.— All proposals of law must be written down, explained, read to the Board of Managers, publicly read and put on the order of the day the last week in the month before discussion.

Art. 16.— The affairs of *administration* and all *urgent* questions are excepted from the operation of this rule.

Art. 17.— In case of opposition, a three-fourths majority will be necessary for an urgency measure.

Art. 18.— Anyone may demand a general discussion before the discussion of each article.

Art. 19.— Each must be uncovered in speaking.

Art. 20.— No one may abstain from voting, either on roll call, or by rising, or by raised hand.

Art. 21.— Each one must state and support his opinion when another member desires to know it.

Art. 22.— No one may abstain from voting in an election.

Art. 23.— The vote on a law as a whole will always be by roll-call.

Art. 24.— It can be taken in the same manner on one or several special articles, when it shall be demanded by the President of the Community or by ten members who rise to that effect.

Art. 25.— The votes are public.

Art. 26.— The vote shall always be by an absolute majority unless a special law be passed providing a quarter majority.

Art. 27.— In the case of an election, when no candidate obtains an absolute majority on the second ballot, the third ballot shall be cast by balloting between the two candidates who have obtained the most in the second.

Art. 28.— The election of the two Vice-Presidents of the Assembly and the three Secretaries will be by rising vote or by raising the hand.

Art. 29.— An outsider may participate in the Assembly only by the authority of the President of the Community.

Art. 30.— The Board of Managers will have a separate table near that of the Assembly Bureau.

Art. 31.— Six commissioners selected from the month's

membership roll, choosing a chairman, are charged with keeping the order of the placing of members, of verifying the late arrivals and those leaving, also the votes and those refraining from voting and all infractions of the present regulation. The Chairman shall make a report which shall be attached to the *process-verbal* and read with the latter to the Assembly.

Art. 32.— Two of the six commissioners will aid the Commissioner of the Refectory to prepare the room before and after the meeting.

Art. 33.— There shall be a special regulation for the preparation of the room, its fuel, its light, etc.

Done at Nauvoo, March 3, 1855.

This project, discussed in three meetings of the General Assembly, was finally carried, on April 22, on roll-call, and adopted by 129 yeas to 2 nays, and became the rule of our General Assembly, replacing the one of January 30, 1851.

THE LAW CONCERNING ADMISSION, WITHDRAWAL AND EXPULSION, OF APRIL 5, 1850.

Admission in America is declared, by the General Assembly, by a three-fourths majority of the voters after verification of the fact that the one requesting unites all qualities and meets all existing conditions of membership.

It is *provisional* or *definitive.*

Provisional admission lasts two months. It is for the *novitiate* to satisfy himself that he really wishes to remain a Community member and that the Community desires him to become so.

If the provisionally admitted one withdraws or is not definitively admitted, he must be given four-fifths of his share brought in, clothes, bed and tools.

He who is admitted definitively can *withdraw.* He will be given one-half of his goods brought in, to wit: 20 dollars and whatever surplus may have resulted from the delay of the General Assembly. They will also return him an outfit of clothing, his bed and tools. He may not demand another thing.

The one who violates the laws and regulations may be *expelled* by a decision of the General Assembly by a three-fourths vote. They will return to him the same as to him who withdraws voluntarily.

But the prosperous condition of the Community having permitted the diminishing of the entrance share and the establishment in Iowa necessitating a new arrangement, I have proposed to the General Assembly the following resolutions which embody the principles of a new law.

PRINCIPLES OF THE REVISION OF THE LAW OF APRIL 5, 1850, UPON ADMISSION, WITHDRAWAL AND EXPULSION.

The President of the Community proposes:

1. To preserve the principle of the novitiate unmodified;

2. To preserve the principle of definitive admission through the *General Assembly* of the Community;

3. To preserve the principle of *optional withdrawal;*

4. To preserve, in case of withdrawal, the principle of the return of a suit of clothing, of a bed and of tools;

5. To preserve, in case of withdrawal from Nauvoo, the principle of the return of one-half of the contributed share conformably to article 26, numbers 4 and 27 of the law of April 5, 1850;

6. To introduce, starting January 1, 1855, a fixed sum for all those who shall not demand one-half of their equal share;

7. To control the question of admitting young girls, admitted without the required shares, that each unmarried man may wish to marry;

8. To reduce to 300 francs the minimum share;

9. To adopt the principle of other successive reductions as soon as possible;

10. To apply as soon as possible the principle of *uniform,* of the *diminishing* of the cost of dress and the replacement of the old dress by a new one which will be furnished by the Community.

SPECIAL ARRANGEMENTS FOR THE COLONY IN IOWA.

The following arrangements are also proposed:

11. All Icarians definitively admitted into the Community, *will be permitted* to leave for the Colony when they so *demand.*

12. The order in which the departure shall be effected will be regulated, among all who demand, by the General Assembly.

13. The one who shall desire to leave shall deliver to the Board of Managers, to be submitted to the General Assembly, his written and signed demand in which he shall promise: 1. to practice more and more the *principles* of the Icarian Community; 2. to observe the Icarian Constitution and all the laws which are and *will be* made by the General Assembly of the Community, notably the law of *May* 28, 1854 on the organization of the Colony, and the present law of June 12, 1854; 3. to not leave the Colony before *two years* without the authorization of the General Assembly; 4. to return to Nauvoo when called by the General Assembly; 5. to demand nothing for his *work* in case of withdrawal and demand only that which is allowed by articles 15 and 16 of the present law; 6. to address himself exclusively to the General Assembly for all *claims or disputes* which may arise against the Colony, the Community, or one of the members.

14. Through an exception to number three of the preceding article, *young men* may, after a year of sojourn in the Colony, be permitted by the General Assembly to return to Nauvoo.

15. The one who shall fraternally leave the Colony before the two years of sojourn, shall receive his suit of clothes and his bed, such as he shall find it at the time of his withdrawal, and the tools which shall have been recognized before his departure as being necessary, or their total value, if the colony judges them indispensable for itself, and beyond that a fixed sum.

16. He who fraternally leaves after the two years, shall receive, beyond the things and the fixed sum arranged by the preceding article the sum of....................dollars, and half for each child above ten years.

17. The present arrangements apply to those who have been admitted before April 5, 1850, and to those who shall arrive at Nauvoo after January 1, 1855; but they cannot have retroactive effect prejudicial to those who have arrived in the Community after the law of April 5, 1850, or who have arrived before January 1, 1855.

Consequently, in case of withdrawal, either from Nauvoo, or from the Colony, they may demand the application of the law of April 5, 1850, if they shall not have voluntarily renounced its privileges.

These arrangements were adopted on June 12, 1854, after several meetings for discussion, on roll-call, by 104 yeas against 5 nays, and 5 abstaining.

CONDITIONS OF ADMISSION.

These are found in the Prospectus. They are here presented in abridged form only:

1. Know well the Icarian writings, have the principles well in mind, and be acquainted with: *The Journey in Icaria; Why I Am a Communist; The Communist Creed; True Christianity; The Colony or Icarian Republic; The Prospectus of 1852.*

2. Be generally able to read and write.

3. Completely adopt the Icarian system.

4 and 5. Devote one's self to the cause of humanity, women and children.

6 to 10. Adopt the principles of *Fraternity, Equality, Communism* and *Unity.*

12 and 13. Surrender *all* property, hiding nothing.

14. Bring *at least* 400 francs or $80.00 (one-half as much for every child under seven years), with his clothing, bed and tools.

15 to 18. Generally follow a useful trade. Able to work in one of the workshops.

19 to 37. Be industrious, vigorous, not too old, of good hearing and temperament, not using tobacco or strong liquors, trained to propriety, decent in words and acts, careful and economical.

38. Agree to marry.

39. Adopt True Christianity as a religion.

40 and 41. Agree to never be hostile toward the Community.

42 to 44. Guarantee that his wife and children have all the necessary qualities.

45. Consent to whatever means the Community may adopt for the education of his children.

46. Accept the Constitution and Laws already made.

THE LAW FOR ORGANIZING THE IOWA COLONY.

Art. 1.— The seat of the Icarian Community is at Nauvoo, Illinois, unless the Community itself may transfer it elsewhere.

Art. 2.— The establishment founded by the Icarian Community in Iowa is, by report to the Community, a *movable workshop,* a *trust,* an *advance-guard,* a *colony.*

Art. 3.— The Colony must apply and practice all principles of Icarian Communism, in order to realize the aim of the Icarian Community.

Art. 4.— Sent out by the Community, founded by it at its expense and for this, the Colony must act, work, produce, pre-empt, acquire and possess for the Community.

Art. 5.— It is under the Community's direction and must execute its Constitution and its Laws made and to be made, its rules and its decisions.

Art. 6.— The Community forbids the passage of any new law or revision of a law, or any change in the constituted principles of the Icarian Community.

Art. 7.— An extract from the act of incorporation granted by the Constitution, shall be repeatedly recorded or publicly registered with the present law in Adams County.

Art. 8.— The Colony must keep a journal of financial proceedings and an account of its operations and work, and render an account of all its receipts and expenditures to the Community.

Art. 9.— It shall write the Community at least once per month.

Art. 10.— The Colony shall meet in a Colonial Assembly to regulate its work and its special operations. The women and young men assist with a consultative voice.

Art. 11.— The Colony may neither make, purchase nor sell furniture, nor begin anything. The Community alone has the right to do this and in its own name. The Colony may not even countenance anything begun within it, except with the permission of the Community, in the name of the latter, with the warning that it will have to surrender it with no return therefor.

Art. 12.— The Colonial Assembly shall have a *President,* a *Vice-President,* and one or two *Secretaries* elected by it for three months.

Art. 13.— The Colony shall have a Director, an Assistant Director, and a Secretary-Treasurer, elected by it, each year and reëligible.

Art. 14.— The election of the Director, Assistant Director and Secretary-Treasurer is subject to the ratification of the General Assembly of the Community.

Art. 15.— The new Director, Assistant Director and Secretaries may enter upon the duties of their offices only after confirmation by the General Assembly of the Community.

Art. 16.— The Director is especially charged with overseeing the execution of the laws of the Community and the observation of its principles, administering the Colony in concert with the Colonial Assembly, executing the decisions of the latter, representing it on the outside and rendering an account of its operations, and corresponding with the Board of Managers.

Art. 17.— The Secretary-Treasurer takes care of the cash, makes the payments, keeps the account books and draws up the letters sent to the Assembly for approval, all of which is under the supervision of the Director, and in collaboration with him.

Art. 18.— Admission to the Colony, the agreements made, the duties of the colonists, all questions relative to the shares will be regulated by special law which will be done by constantly revising the law of April 5, 1850, on admission, withdrawal, and expulsion, and for the regulation of what shall be given the one or the other who shall leave, either from the Community or from the Colony.

Art. 19.— When the Colony shall include a majority of people definitely admitted into the community — the seat of the latter shall be transferred to the Colony, by a law which shall regulate the organization or the action of the minority, or of the rear-guard remaining at Nauvoo.

This was presented by Citizen Cabet, May 6, discussed in

five meetings, and adopted May 28, upon roll-call, by two hundred to twelve.

Done at Nauvoo, May 28, 1854.

APPEAL TO ICARIANS OF EUROPE AND AMERICA AND TO PHILANTHROPISTS

Icarians of all countries, who are well acquainted with our Icarian system and our Icarian doctrine, who adopt them completely, who partake of our devotion to the cause of the People and of Humanity, who combine all the necessary qualities, who fill all the required conditions, and especially who consent freely and voluntarily to put all in common in order to bring about the triumph of our system of Fraternity and Community, Equality and Liberty, of Democracy and of the Republic, come, aid us to establish in the wilderness an Icarian Commune and afterward a State. Come, Brothers, and you will be welcome!

And you who can not come, but who have heroic spirits and generous hearts, you, friends of Progress and of Humanity, you Philosophers or Philanthropists of all classes, you sincere and zealous Christians who desire to contribute by your works to the realization of the true principles of Christianity, you philanthropic Societies, aid us with all your strength and all your means, in our great and difficult evangelical and humanitarian enterprise!

We have everything to create in the wilderness, our houses and our workshops, our agriculture and our industry; our sciences and our arts, our schools and our temples; we shall have need of land and of animals, of machines and of steamboats, etc. etc., that is to say, of money and of much money. Assist us by your knowledge and your advice, by your support, above all by your gifts or your loans.

There are many wealthy people who desire to make themselves useful without knowing how to satisfy their desires effectually. Let them promote the success of Icaria and the grateful Icarians will perpetuate their names as benefactors of Humanity.

The President of the Community.

CABET.